Thomas More
The King's Good Servant

Written by Dorothy Smith

Illustrated by Robert Broomfield

PAULIST PRESS
New York/New Jersey

For Alice Jessie Lilian Dorothy
with love

First published in Great Britain in 1988 by McCrimmon
Publishing Co Ltd, Great Wakering Essex England. Published
in 1990 in the United States of America by Paulist Press,
997 Macarthur Boulevard, Mahwah, New Jersey 07430.

Library of Congress Cataloging-in-Publication Data

Smith, Dorothy.
    Thomas More: the king's good servant/by Dorothy Smith.
        p. cm.
    Illustrated by Robert Broomfield.
    Summary: Examines the life of the sixteenth-century English
scholar and statesman whose clash of wills with Henry the
Eighth led to his execution and eventual canonization.
    ISBN 0-8091-6595-3
    1. More, Thomas, Sir, Saint, 1478–1535—Juvenile
literature. 2. Statesmen—Great Britain—Biography—Juvenile
literature. 3. Humanists—Great Britain—Biography—Juvenile
literature. 4. Christian martyrs—Great Britain—Biography—
Juvenile literature. 5. Great Britain—History—Henry VIII,
1509–1547—Juvenile literature. [1. More, Thomas, Sir, Saint,
1478–1535. 2. Statesmen. 3. Saints.] I. Broomfield,
Robert, 1930–   ill. II. Title.
DA334.M8S56   1990
942.05′2′092—dc20   89-49287
[B]   CIP
                                                           AC

Cover design Robert Broomfield

Printed in Hong Kong.

Contents

1. *A man for all seasons*

THOMAS More had a loving family and a great many friends, who all enjoyed his company. One of these friends declared that Thomas More was 'a man for all seasons', and these words fit him so well that a famous play and a film have been made about him, called just that—*A Man For All Seasons.*

His friend meant that More was an all-round, complete man. He would sit with his friends after dinner, talking and joking, then he would change and his conversation would become grave and serious. He loved his large family, children, adopted children and grandchildren, but he could leave the family hearth and go to court, where his opinions were asked for by the King himself. He lived in the world, and held one of the highest offices in the kingdom, and he enjoyed every part of his life. Yet more than everything else, he loved God. He believed that there was much wrong with the Church, which he would have liked to have seen put right, but in the end he died for it. He gave up everything else—his family and friends, his home, his writings, to carry out what he firmly believed was God's purpose for him.

Often we feel that many of the saints were very splendid, but they would have been rather uncomfortable to have around. Thomas More, the popular guest and the friendly host, was a saint whom everyone liked—even his enemies. So . . . Thomas More, the Man For All Seasons, was a nice man, and a brave man, who died for something he believed to be right. Hundreds of years afterwards, he is still a saint many people would like to have known.

2. A boy growing up

THE BOY Thomas was the son of a well known lawyer called John More and his wife Isabel, and the family lived in Cheapside, in the City of London, more than five hundred years ago.

England was a wild dangerous place then, for mighty barons with private armies took up arms against each other. Ordinary people were hardly involved in the struggle, but they saw the country torn in pieces by the Wars of the Roses. Followers of the House of York, with a white rose for their badge, were clutched in a death-struggle with the House of Lancaster, who had taken a red rose, as each tried to put their own candidate on the throne as king. As the English men and women saw villages burned, crops stolen and horses carried off for the war, they felt they would be happy to see *any* king on the throne, so long as he could bring peace and order.

The City of London was the home of merchants and bankers, as well as lawyers; and as both sides needed their money, the City was not too much damaged by fighting. The More family had a comfortable house and lived well, and they had a country house in Hertfordshire, about twenty-five miles away. Thomas was expected to become a lawyer like his father, for at that time boys usually followed the same trade or profession as their fathers; so he was sent to a school where he would be well educated.

Schools were strange places in those days. They were meant only for boys. If girls were educated at all, they were taught at home, or picked up what they could; but many women from good and prosperous families could not even read or write. All they were expected to know was how to run their households well.

At school, once the boys knew their letters, they were taught in Latin—Latin all the time. This was not the classical Latin that had been written and spoken by the Romans, but a kind of 'Church' Latin, that was spoken by educated men all over Europe, and used for official business as well as for church services. Schoolboys learnt to translate Latin, to read Latin, to write it, to make speeches in it, to argue in Latin in debates with the other boys. It might have been useful later on, but it was desperately dull at the time, as there was nothing else—no reading books in English, no history or geography, or even mathematics or science. Printed books were very rare and very expensive, so many of the lessons consisted of learning everything by heart, or laboriously writing down exactly what the master told them.

Thomas learnt his Latin at St Anthony's School in Threadneedle Street, which was well known for giving boys a good beginning to their education. Thomas was a clever boy and got on well at his lessons. The school was close to his home in Cheapside, so he probably crept round there on the dark winter mornings, and hurried home cheerfully when the long school day was over.

When Thomas was just getting started at school, when he was about eight, in 1485, life improved for the people of England as the long drawn out Wars of the Roses came to an end and a new king came to the throne. His name was Henry Tudor, and he took the title of King Henry VII. He said he was determined to bring peace and order to the war-torn country. Thomas More's life was spent under the Tudor monarchy, Henry VII and his son, Henry VIII.

When Thomas was twelve, his father took him from school and sent him as a page boy to the household of the Archbishop of Canterbury, Cardinal Morton. This was a common step for promising boys of prosperous families; they carried on with their lessons, and at the same time they had duties in the household. They waited at table, announced the master's guests, waited on them and ran errands. If the master was a great man, a noble or an official at court, the boys met a great many important people, who might employ them later on. They learned court etiquette and good manners, and how lords and ladies should be spoken to, so that they would know how to behave when they took their own places in the world.

Naturally the Archbishop of Canterbury was a very important man, in the King's government as well as in the Church. Cardinal Morton was Lord Chancellor of England, which meant he was the chief official in the kingdom; so John More was behaving as a very far-sighted father when he got the young Thomas a place in his household. Thomas saw all the great men of England, as well as ambassadors from foreign countries, when they came to see Cardinal Morton at Lambeth Palace, and he would listen in silence as they talked about state affairs. Later on, everyone spoke of Thomas's polished friendly manners; they were learnt in these years, as well as coming from his own friendly nature.

The page boys in any big household were usually a lively set, who enjoyed life. Although they still had lessons, it was better than the long hours and rigid pattern of school, and they felt they were seeing life, and they had many chances for fun. They were allowed to join in official festivities, too, for the Cardinal entertained his guests lavishly,

and the pages were required to attend on them. At Christmas and other festivals there would be musicians, and companies of players to entertain them. Thomas loved the players, and sometimes he even joined them and took a part in the play. He was said to be clever and funny.

Cardinal Morton himself noticed the bright-eyed intelligent boy, listening to every word that was said, and pointed him out to his guests, saying 'Who ever shall live till then will see that this child here waiting at table, will turn out to be a marvellous man.'

Thomas learned a great deal in Cardinal Morton's household, but he was only there for two years, for Cardinal Morton thought then that the boy was

ready for the university, and John More agreed. He was still young, only fourteen, but it was the custom for boys to go to the university much earlier then, and they both thought he would benefit from it. With Cardinal Morton to speak for him, he was quickly accepted, and went to Canterbury College, which later became part of Christ Church in the University of Oxford.

Once there, the life of the schoolboy in the lawyer's comfortable family house, or the life of the lively page boy in luxurious Lambeth Palace, changed dramatically. Students at Oxford were young, and very strictly controlled by their tutor. Life was hard, with a great deal of work and no comforts, and they had no way of enjoying themselves unless their fathers gave them the money for it. John More had no intention of increasing his son's allowance, for he believed that if he had no money to spend, he could not do anything but study hard. So, often cold, hungry and down at heel—for he had not even the money to get his boots repaired, unless his father sent it—young Thomas More spent two years at Oxford.

Then his father decided that if he was to follow in his footsteps and become a lawyer, it was time for Thomas to leave Oxford and become a law student. So in 1496 he enrolled at New Inn, and later went to Lincoln's Inn.

Now, at last, as a trained young lawyer, educated at a good school and at Oxford, polished and experienced in the ways and customs of a great man's household, seen by everyone as a young man of great promise, Thomas More was ready to take his place in the world.

3. *The New Learning and the New Age*

WHEN Henry Tudor became King Henry VII in 1485, he brought the Wars of the Roses to an end. But that was not all. He made a new beginning, so that his reign was seen as ending in England the time that is called the Middle Ages, stretching between the ancient world of Greece and Rome and what we call modern times. In England, 'modern history' begins with Henry VII in 1485. Of course everything did not change suddenly, on a certain date; but great changes were going on in every part of life.

It was not just because the Civil War was over, and a new king was on the throne. The peace and order he brought gave people a chance to look out and see what was happening in the world, in Europe as well as in their own country. Such mighty changes were happening that they called the time a New Birth—a Renaissance.

The Middle Ages were an age of faith. All men and women belonged to the Church and believed what the Church taught them without questioning.

Now they began to question—everything. It was an age of Enquiry, an age of Discovery, as if men realised there was a world outside their own country, outside their own times. No longer need ships continuously hug the coast or creep across the Channel—they could make great voyages across the deep ocean, to find new worlds beyond the seas. Thomas More was fifteen years old when Columbus first reached America.

In the world of the mind, too, men began to make uncharted voyages. No longer was all history contained in the centuries of the Christian era, or all knowledge in the writings of the fathers of the Church. Before that time, leading up to it, the history of Greece and of Rome showed the deep roots that all men shared. No longer was the only language worth learning the rough and ready Latin simplified by churchmen: within reach was the pure classical Latin, and beyond that there was Greek; and in both languages there were writers, philosophers, poets, who had been unknown for a thousand years. Even the scriptures, the gospels and epistles of the New Testament, had first been written down in Greek. To learn more of the ancient tongues was to learn more about the beginnings of Christianity itself.

Artists were caught up in the new enthusiasm. They no longer painted flat figures of the saints but real men and women, sometimes as models for holy pictures, sometimes as the gods and goddesses in Greek and Roman stories. Paintings of Our Lady and the baby Jesus were really paintings of a young mother and her baby. Sometimes the artists did not pretend their sitters were anybody else, but painted them as they were, as portraits, real people in real clothes, sitting in the houses where they actually lived.

Other men—scientists, we might call them, though the word was not known then—tried to find out more about the natural world. How did the bodies of men and women work? How did the stars follow their patterns in the sky? Men like Leonardo da Vinci—except that there never was another man like Leonardo da Vinci!—dreamt of machines that could fly like a bird.

When More first went to school, printed books were rare and expensive. Now every year more books were printed, and moved around among scholars, so that the New Learning was in the reach of more people. Most of the population still could not read or write, but even that was changing year by year.

So with the beginning of a new century, after 1500, young people felt they were living in a great new age—an age of discovery, a discovery of the Old World, a discovery of the New World, a discovery of Man. Thomas More was twenty-two as the new century opened, and he was seen as a man of the new age.

The new learning had reached Oxford, so that More met scholars there learned in Greek, and attended some of their lectures. He began to realise the existence of philosophers and ideas, plays and playwrights that he had never dreamed of; but he was very young in his Oxford years, and did not pursue them. He was fascinated by them, though, and after he returned to London, as a young law student he continued his studies on his own and with a growing group of friends who shared all these interests, who used to meet and talk together.

More's greatest friend was not an Englishman but a Dutch scholar, who was known through Europe as Erasmus. They met in 1499, when More was twenty-one years old, and they were friends for more than thirty years. Though very learned, Erasmus was a bitter, unhappy man, and he found More's serenity and cheerfulness particularly comforting. 'What did nature ever create milder, sweeter or happier than the mind of Thomas More?' he wrote.

Erasmus moved from one university to another, right across Europe. He used to say that the mule he rode on was the most learned animal in Europe, since it did nothing but travel from one university to the next! More's professional duties kept him tied to London and the centre of affairs, but Erasmus visited More whenever he came to England and they wrote long letters to each other, discussing everything and setting out how they would put right all the evils in the world. They believed that the Church itself needed reforms, to rid it of badly educated clergy, or corrupt clergy who got rich out of money given by the faithful; and they wanted to reform the monasteries and make them once more centres of religious life.

Once, while he was staying with More, Erasmus wrote a book mocking all the evils he saw in the world and in the Church. In English the book is called In Praise of Folly, but the book was written in Latin, and its title is a joke—*ENCOMIUM MORIAE*, which also means In Praise of More!

4. Life at Chelsea

IN HIS early years in London, More not only studied law, but Greek and theology as well. He lived at Charterhouse, the London monastery of a very strict order which had not relaxed or gone soft, as many of the monasteries were accused of doing. He allowed himself little food or sleep. In later years, when people were amazed at how little sleep he needed, he said it was a habit he had learnt during these years.

For a while he believed strongly that he should take Holy Orders himself, and enter the Church as a priest. Eventually he decided against it. He felt he could serve God in the world by working at his profession and using his influence there, and by marrying and having a family.

In 1505 he married a lady named Jane Colt. She was clever and intelligent, but like most women she had received very little education. It was a delight to More to teach her about books and music, though Jane herself, newly married, with a house to run, and before long with four small children, progressed only slowly. Then, sadly, she died still in her early twenties, leaving three little girls, called Margaret,

Elizabeth and Cecily, and a son named John. Very
soon More married again, a lady who was always
known as Dame Alice, a widow with a little girl
of her own. More married her to look after his
children and his household; he was not in love with
her, and indeed he said: 'She is neither a pearl nor
a girl!' But though his friends were always rather
nervous of her sharp tongue, More respected all her
good qualities and became very fond of her in their
twenty-five-year-long marriage.

With his own four children, Dame Alice's daughter, and several adopted children, More was now the head of a large family. He worked hard as a lawyer to support them all, but when they were young he always had time to oversee their lessons, even when he had no time to teach them himself. He wrote letters in Latin to his children when they were quite young, nearly every day, and he expected them to write him good letters in reply. He wanted even his daughters to be educated. It was so rare for girls to be taught anything in those days that Thomas More's daughters, who knew Greek as well as Latin, became famous, as if they were animals who could perform clever tricks. The eldest daughter, Margaret, called Meg, was particularly dear to More, and he believed that she could really have been a great scholar.

When the children were young, More and his family lived in the City of London. As he grew richer, and the family larger, he moved to a new house just out of London, on the river at Chelsea, which was a tiny village in those days. So many people visited the house at Chelsea, and described it, that we have a clear picture of them all, family and friends, living there. Thomas More at Chelsea is famous, like Shakespeare at Stratford-on-Avon or the Brontes at Haworth.

It was a household based on religion and learning. All the family read books and studied, and wrote letters in elegant Latin. Every member was involved with family prayer, as well as private prayers and religious reading. Part of the house was known as the New Building: there More himself passed many hours in religious study and meditation, and he spent all day there on Fridays, in a kind of retreat. Though he believed some things in the churches should be improved, this did not weaken in his own faith.

One welcome guest was Hans Holbein, a portrait painter from Germany. He said the house was 'dignified without being magnificent'. He was commissioned to paint portraits of all the family, separately and as a family group. The paintings he made, and the delightful lively sketches he worked from, are so full of character and personality that we really see the More family just as they were, in the clothes they wore and the house they lived in. All this emphasis on the importance of each person as a

Thomas More and family
after Holbein

separate individual is part of the spirit of the New Age, of Discovery and of the New Learning. In the big family group, even the ladies are holding books in their hands, which they are reading or talking about, and Sir John More, the wise father who became a respected judge, sits next to his distinguished son.

A pen and ink sketch of the family group was sent as a present to Erasmus, who was overjoyed.

After Margaret married a man called Thomas Roper, she and her husband still lived in the house in Chelsea, together with their children, More's grandchildren. When Margaret was expecting her

first baby, her father wrote to her in Latin: 'May God and our Blessed Lady grant you happily and safely an addition to your family like to his mother in everything except sex. Let it indeed be a girl, if she will make up for the disadvantage of her sex by her zeal to emulate her mother's virtue and learning. I would most certainly prefer such a girl to three boys!'

The household always included a great many animals, for More loved strange beasts of all kinds. At different times he owned monkeys, a fox, a weasel and a beaver, as well as assorted rabbits.

More loved to entertain his friends at Chelsea, where the food was plentiful but plain. He was ready to help anyone in trouble, and created a happy atmosphere where his family and friends could be at ease together. A friend named Richard Whittinton wrote a book of essays, in English, to be translated into Latin by students. One of them contained the famous description of Thomas More. He said:

> 'More is a man of angel's wit and singular learning. I know not his fellow. For where is the man of that gentleness, lowliness and affability? And as time requires, a man of marvellous mirth and pastimes, and sometimes of as sad gravity. A man for all seasons'.

5. *Utopia*

A S WELL as being a lawyer and a scholar, Thomas More was famous as a writer. By far his best known book was called *Utopia,* which he wrote in Latin in 1516. It was popular at once, and it has been read—translated into English and many other languages—in all the hundreds of years since then. It gave a new word to the language—*Utopian* which means 'belonging to an ideal country'.

The book is about an unknown country; a country that never was. More lived in an age of discovery, when new lands were being discovered; all North and South America, all the southern half of Africa, countless unknown islands, had been revealed in More's own lifetime. People were amazed by all the travellers' tales, and readers were in the mood to read about another, even stranger country. It was just like today, when space travel and new technology have given people an appetite for science fiction in books and films.

Utopia was a strange society. Its citizens owned no property, and their houses and gardens belonged to them all in common. They used no money; all the

goods and food they produced were stored in ware-
houses, and the head of every household was free to
take without charge whatever his family needed.
They worked for only three hours in the morning,
and another three later in the day. With all the
citizens working, this was enough to provide for all
their needs. The rest of the time they spent in lei-
sure, in music or learning.

All meals were taken together, in communal
dining halls, while someone read aloud to them.
They allowed no hunting, for they took no pleasure
in seeing 'a silly innocent hare murdered by a dog'.
The sick and aged were well cared for; but a citizen
in great pain could arrange to end his own life if he
so desired.

The Utopians were not Christians, but they wor-
shipped a godly power which they called 'the Father
of All'; and women as well as men could become
priests of this religion. They believed in a happy life
after death.

Readers have never been sure if Thomas More
was laughing at his own times when he wrote about
Utopia, or if he thought it was a perfect society
which ought to be imitated. It is clear he admired
the Utopians for their serenity, and the calm way
their society was arranged. It is certain, too, that he
got a great deal of amusement from writing his most
famous book!

6. *The young King*

THOMAS More and his friends looked to a bright future for the country, and to the coming of better days. It was a time of great hopefulness. The Wars of the Roses had done great harm; Henry VII had restored law and order, but he had ruled harshly and imposed heavy taxes on all his subjects. More himself had opposed the King, as a member of Parliament; and though he had won and the tax was not imposed, the King was very angry with him. It was clear his prospects were poor so long as Henry VII was still king.

Henry VII was seen as a tired old man of the past century. When he died in 1509, it was the dawn of a new age to match the new century. His eldest son Arthur had died a few years before, when he was only sixteen years old, so his second son became king, as King Henry VIII.

We know exactly what he looked like. Holbein became his court painter, and his portraits are famous—we know them well. Henry VIII was broad, solid, four square, staring out at the world with confident, rather small eyes, determined to get what he wanted out of life. These portraits were painted when Henry was middle-aged, fat, and accustomed to rule without any opposition. When he became King he was only seventeen years old, tall, athletic and handsome, his red gold hair shining like the sun. He loved games and sports, running and wrestling and the game of real tennis.

The Venetian ambassador described him: 'His Majesty is extremely handsome. Nature could not have done more for him, he is much handsomer than any other sovereign in Christendom; a great deal handsomer than the King of France, very fair and his whole frame admirably proportioned. He has allowed his beard to grow, and as it is reddish, he has now got a beard that looks like gold. He is extemely fond of tennis, and it is the prettiest thing in the world to see him play, his fair skin glowing through a shirt of the finest texture.'

Yet he enjoyed serious reading, too, and was a student of the New Learning. 'Heaven laughs and the earth rejoices,' a friend wrote to Erasmus. 'Our king is not after gold, or gems, or precious metals, but virtue, glory, immortality.'

The disastrous Wars of the Roses had been a very bad time, with armies fighting while two or more men claimed to be king at once. The land fell into poverty and misery. When the wars ended, men were determined the country should not know such bad times again. The best thing seemed to be to have a strong king—so Henry VII, and Henry VIII even more so, were obeyed without question, flattered and never opposed. The kings got stronger and stronger, and soon they really could do as they wished, so that people were afraid of them. This lasted all the time the Tudors were on the throne, Henry VII, and his son, and his grandchildren.

Young Henry was determined to rule well, in the place of his brother Arthur who had died. Though so young, Arther had already been married to a Spanish Princess, known as Catherine of Aragon. Since Arthur's death she had lived as a widow in England, and now she was twenty-two years old. Henry got special permission from the Pope to marry his brother's widow; so Henry and Catherine were married, and they were very happy together. To keep the throne secure, it was very important that Henry should have sons, so that there would be a clear heir. Henry was as determined as his father had been to establish a royal House of Tudor to rule England for many years to come.

Yet Henry was not as wise as his father; for while Henry VII hated to spend money, but wanted to make the crown rich and powerful, Henry was ready to spend it on anything to make a show—on a rich and spendid court, on ships, on armies to make himself powerful abroad.

Henry had a great admiration for Thomas More and asked him to go to court, and to take an active part in public affairs and in politics. More was doubtful for a long while: it would mean giving up many of his hours of study; it would mean that he would see less of his family. Even worse, he feared he would have to give up the hours he devoted to his prayers and religious duties. But a king's 'request' cannot be refused for ever, and at last Thomas More became the servant of King Henry VIII. He was first a member of the King's Council, accepting special missions to countries overseas.

Erasmus regretted the change, though he could see there was no help for it. 'The one thing that consoles me about your going to court is that it is under the best of kings; still, you are lost to us and learning,' he said.

The King's chief minister, the Lord Chancellor, was Cardinal Wolsey. He was an immensely powerful man, head of the government, head of the church, a strong figure in dealing with all the kings and rulers of Europe, with tremendous influence on the young King. In the early years Henry wanted all the show of being a king, but did not enjoy the hard work. So Wolsey worked, and became enormously rich. He built himself a fine palace, far grander than anything the king possessed. It still exists, and is called Hampton Court.

Wolsey could have used his power and influence to make changes and reforms in the Church, such as More and his friends wanted. But he did not want to stir up trouble, or have questions asked about his own wealth, so he let matters slide from bad to worse.

In 1520, Wolsey organised a summit meeting between Henry VIII and Francis I, King of France. It was so lavish and splendid, it was known as the Field of the Cloth of Gold. As one of the King's councillors, More went to France and saw all the splendid and historic spectacle. In honour of this event he was knighted that year, and became *Sir* Thomas More.

Often the king would send for Sir Thomas to discuss Greek, or theology, or astronomy, or anything else that he was interested in. Sometimes he would even make a surprise visit to the house in Chelsea, and walk with Sir Thomas in the garden, like a friend. Roper, his son-in-law, congratulated him on these marks of royal favour; but Thomas More knew how much reliance an ordinary man can put upon a king's friendship.

'I have no cause to be proud of it, son Roper,' he said, 'for if my head could win him a castle in France, it should not fail to go!'

7. *Defender of the Faith*

THE YOUNG king prided himself on his knowledge of the Scriptures, and of his loyalty to the doctrines of the Church. He enjoyed conversation with such a noted theologian as Sir Thomas, and liked to feel he was able to give a good account of himself in their discussions.

The King and his adviser were both disturbed by news coming from Germany about a monk named Martin Luther. Like More and Erasmus, and many others, he saw a great need for reform in the Church; but when the reforms were slow to come, and the Church and its bishops showed no readiness to put their own house in order, Luther took a desperate step. He gave up his vows as a monk and declared that the authority of the Pope was imposed unlawfully on the Church and on Christians. They should, he said *PROTEST* against his rule and set up their own church. It would be based on reading the Bible and their own consciences, not on teaching passed down by the Pope and bishops.

In Germany and elsewhere, many men, in despair at the corruption of the Church, and seeing no hope of reform, followed Luther. They were called *PROTESTANTS*.

Luther not only denied the rule of the Pope; he questioned the actual teaching of the Church. He said that not all the seven sacraments had actually been given by Christ himself. A Christian needed only Baptism and Holy Communion for his salvation.

Thomas More believed that reforms were a good thing, but he could see that a split in the Church could do enormous harm. He wanted to keep the Church united—reformed if possible, but united at all costs.

Henry was appalled by all Luther's teaching, and wanted to stand up against it. He wrote a book, called *Assertion of the SEVEN Sacraments*; he consulted English Scholars, including Sir Thomas More, who was known as a reformer as well as devoted to the Church, like the King himself. Although he made use of advisers, Henry was very anxious that the book should be regarded as all his own work.

Indeed, Sir Thomas More himself was doubtful whether the King was wise to stress the authority of the Pope so positively. 'I think it best that his authority be more slenderly touched,' he said.

The King refused to make any alterations. 'We are so much bound to the See of Rome that we cannot do too much honour to it,' he insisted.

Luther was furious when he read the book, and wrote a coarse and angry pamphlet against it. On Henry's orders, More replied to it in the same style. The Pope, on the other hand, was delighted that the King of England had defended him so vigorously. Gratefully, he wanted to confer some honour on

Henry, so he awarded him the title Defender of the Faith (in Latin, *Fidei Defensor*).

Henry was overjoyed. He used the title all his life, and passed it on to the rulers who came after him. Even today, four hundred and fifty years later, our present Queen has *Fid Def* engraved on all the coins of the realm.

8. *The King's divorce*

OR THE FIRST fifteen years that Henry
ruled as King, he was greatly admired by his
courtiers and officials and very popular with
the ordinary folk of England. Government was in
the powerful hands of Cardinal Wolsey, and if he
became every year richer and more proud, and less
popular, still he left Henry free for his sports and
his studies.

Yet after fifteen years, a worry at the back of
Henry's mind grew larger, and would not go away.
He had been happy with his wife Catherine, who
was a good and intelligent woman, but they had a
great sorrow—they had no son. Catherine had had
seven children, but only one had lived, the Princess
Mary, who was born in 1516.

Now Henry was deeply worried about who would
be King after him. His father had made himself
King after the country had been torn by bitter years
of civil war. Henry VII, and Henry VIII after him,
believed that the Tudor kings must be strong and
powerful, to give peace and good government to the
country. In England it was possible, by law, for a
woman to rule; but it had happened only once, cen-

turies before, and no one wanted to see that disaster repeated.

So Henry needed a son, and he believed England needed a son. He looked back on his marriage to Catherine, who had once been the wife of his brother Arthur. The Pope had given permission for Henry and Catherine to marry—but suppose the Pope had no right to do so? Was God angry with Henry for a marriage that was against his law? Was *that* why there was no son to succeed him?

Henry believed he should end his marriage to Catherine and marry again. Then there would be a prince to succeed him. So he asked the Pope for his permission to divorce Catherine. The Catholic Church did not allow divorce; but in special cases, among royalty, for the public good, or to make sure of an heir to the throne, it had sometimes been allowed. The Pope sent Cardinal Campeggio to England and said the case should be decided by him and Cardinal Wolsey.

Cardinal Wolsey believed that if the divorce went through, Henry should make an important marriage with a French princess. But Henry had no such intention. He had fallen in love with a beautiful young English woman, named Anne Boleyn, and though she was not royal he was determined to marry her. Anne was determined, too. She was very ambitious, and she dreamed of becoming Queen and having a son who would be King.

After many delays, the Pope declared that he would hear the case himself, in Rome, which would obviously lead to *more* delays. Henry was furious. He believed Wolsey had betrayed him by not pushing harder for the divorce. Suddenly he was deeply suspicious of Wolsey's ostentatious riches

and honours. Wolsey quickly tried to hand them over to the King, as a 'gift', but it was too late for him to save himself. He was arrested, charged with treason and ordered to come to London to stand his trial. Before that could happen, Wolsey died on the journey. When we think of the ends that other enemies of Henry were to meet before his reign was over, perhaps Wolsey was lucky.

Now Henry had two problems: he wanted his divorce, and he needed a new Lord Chancellor.

For his Chancellor, Henry wanted a man who was respected in the country, and loyal to himself. He chose Sir Thomas More. It was a strange appointment; for centuries the office of Lord Chancellor had been held by a Prince of the Church. Certainly More was a good and honest man, but he knew there was a problem; he was not in favour of the king's divorce. He had been able to hide his views while Wolsey was in power, and now he begged the King never to use him in putting the divorce forward, against his conscience. Henry promised.

Because of this, More was never a great political figure, as Lord Chancellor, but he was a great judge. He cut down on the long time it took to get cases heard, he gave fair, unbiased judgements, and he refused to take bribes.

The problem of the divorce was not solved so easily, as by now it was clear that the Pope would never grant it. Only twenty years before an earlier Pope had given special permission for the marriage, so at a time when the Pope's authority was being questioned by the Lutherans, it would make nonsense of his position for that permission to be cancelled by another Pope now.

Even more important, Catherine's nephew was the most important man in Europe. He was the Emperor Charles V, and his lands stretched across the Continent and included much of the New World. The Pope was now actually at war with Protestants in many countries and dared not offend this powerful ruler. Charles would have been outraged if the Pope had allowed Henry to set the Emperor's aunt aside by divorcing Catherine.

Yet Henry was determined. *Why* should the Pope refuse his request? He genuinely believed that it would be for the good of the country; and for twenty years no one had denied the King anything. He wanted a son. And he wanted to marry Anne Boleyn. He had always been a good son of the Church, but the Pope was the Bishop of Rome. Why should he have any authority over England and England's King? Henry asked himself.

Now Henry was working out ways of getting a divorce from Catherine. He was ready to set the Pope aside, but he must make sure the English church and its bishops went along with him. He turned for advice to men he knew would support him at any cost, either through fear or for what they might get out of it.

Sir Thomas had no part in this, although he never criticised Henry; but the King no longer thought of himself as Sir Thomas's friend. Anne Boleyn, waiting to marry Henry and become Queen, hated Sir Thomas. He stood in her way, and she was a woman who was quicker to hate than to forgive.

There was something else. Henry had spent a lot of money in the last twenty years. His extravagant life style, and his wars in Europe, had run through the careful savings of his father, Henry VII. When he had pulled Wolsey down, he had taken over his enormous riches and his great palace at Hampton Court. Henry realised he could confiscate the wealth of all his enemies—and the church was very rich.

9. The struggle

THE KING started by calling an assembly of the clergy, and attacking them. He declared that they had all committed great crimes against the King, by accepting the Pope as their overlord and allowing him to decide on matters that affected the Church in England. There were threats against them, and the terrified clergy meekly asked the King's pardon and offered him £100,000 to overlook their so-called offences. That was a vast sum of money in those days.

And what was more, they agreed to accept the King as 'the only Supreme Head of the English Church'.

Fisher, the highly respected Bishop of Rochester, protested at that, though hardly any one else of the clergy made a murmur against it. Henry made a great concession and added the words 'as far as the law of Christ allows'. The clergy gave up any struggle. On May 15th, 1532, they accepted Henry, not the Pope, as Head of the Church in England.

The next day, Thomas More resigned his office as Lord Chancellor of the kingdom, on the grounds of ill health. His heavy gold collar, his badge of office, went back to the King. This made him a poor man; for unlike Wolsey, he had never piled up a fortune when he was in power. He found jobs with friends for his servants and secretaries, and his gold-trimmed official barge, with eight watermen, went to the next Lord Chancellor.

For the time, More and his family carried on living in the house at Chelsea; but he was not sure how long that would last. His wife, Dame Alice, was desperately upset to lose her comforts and to see her deeply admired husband fall on bad times. More himself kept cheerful. He wrote to Erasmus, saying he had lived much worse when he had been an Oxford student; and he was happy that after so many years of being busy, he had more time to give to God.

In January 1533, Henry married Anne Boleyn, declaring that the marriage to Catherine was over. The Pope, who had waited seven years to give a ruling, now said the marriage to Catherine must stand and the marriage to Anne was not legal. He declared Henry to be outside the Church.

Henry and Anne no longer cared. A daughter, Elizabeth, was born to them, and they hoped soon there would be sons. Parliament was ordered to pass an Act of Succession: after Henry, the crown would go to his son, if he had one; if not, to the Princess Elizabeth. Princess Mary, seventeen-year-old daughter of Catherine of Aragon, was completely passed over.

In June 1533, Anne was crowned Queen. Many friends urged More to attend the Coronation and end his opposition to the King, now that it could no longer do any good. But when Anne was crowned in Westminster Abbey, although lords and bishops and officials flocked there to show how *they* supported the King, Thomas did not go. Anne, and Henry too, never forgave him for that.

Henry was now ruling England as a dictator, and Parliament did exactly as he said. In March 1534 a new law declared that anyone who condemned the marriage to Anne, or did not accept the new heirs to the throne, was guilty of treason. The penalty was a horrible death, and all the 'traitor's' possessions went to the King, leaving his family poverty stricken.

Every man in the country could be ordered to take a solemn oath declaring that he supported the Act of Succession, and acknowledged the King as Supreme Head of the Church in England.

So how would that affect Thomas More? He had little time to wonder.

That Easter he was ordered to take the oath in the form the Act demanded, in front of the Archbishop of Canterbury, Thomas Cranmer.

The next day, saying goodbye to his family, he left the house at Chelsea for the last time. Usually he loved them to come with him to the water's edge, and there he would kiss them goodbye. This sad time he said goodbye in the house, and told them all not to follow him. He strode through the garden and closed the gate firmly behind him, entered a boat and set out for Lambeth Palace. Roper, his son-in-law, Meg's husband, was with him. For a while he was quite silent; then suddenly he exclaimed: 'Son Roper, I thank Our Lord, the field is won!'

Saying goodbye to his family was for him the hardest part, but he still had a long hard path before him. The matter had now gone beyond the question of the divorce, or the marriage and coronation of Anne Boleyn. Perhaps it had even gone beyond the question of the Pope's authority, but turned on Henry's absolute power.

Archbishop Cranmer told More: 'For a certainty and a thing without doubt, you should obey your sovereign Lord your King.'

'Not in all things,' insisted More's conscience. 'If I know, from God's voice telling me, that a thing is wrong, it is not right because the King commands it.'

More was prepared to accept the Act of Succession, saying that it was the business of the King and Parliament to decide on who would rule after Henry. But he refused to take the Oath of Supremacy, without stating his reasons.

Bishop Fisher had taken the same point of view; and the two men, who had grown old serving Church and State, were sent as prisoners to the Tower in April 1534.

More was calm and resigned. He was allowed books and writing materials, and he spent time writing a book himself, called *Dialogue of Comfort in Tribulation*. He was allowed visits from Meg and Roper, and from Dame Alice; but these were painful, for he knew his enemies hoped they would persuade him to change his mind, and they had no idea why he was acting as he did. He refused to tell them; he would not appear to condemn the King, nor seem to persuade his family to break the law.

When his family were upset during their visits, he tried to comfort them with a little joke. 'Is not this house as near to Heaven as my own?' he asked them.

At last Meg gave up trying to persuade him, and

wrote: 'We live in hope that we shall soon receive you at home again. I pray God heartily that we may, if it be his holy will.'

He was often questioned by officials, including Richard Rich, the Solicitor General; some of them hoped to persuade him to obey the king, while others hoped to trap him so that he could be charged with treason. All the time he refused to

take the oath, and refused to give his reasons for refusing.

For seven months he lay in the Tower, not brought to trial, not set free. Then he received a sinister message from the King's secretary, Thomas Cromwell. 'Master Secretary sends you word, as your true friend, to remember that Parliament still lasts.' And indeed Parliament was still sitting, passing laws as the King commanded. When Parliament met again, an Act was passed sentencing More, without any trial, to life imprisonment, and all his goods were confiscated. His imprisonment grew harsher. His books were removed and the few comforts in his cell taken away.

Today, thousands of sightseers every year visit the Tower of London. They admire the Crown Jewels, the Yeomen of the Guard, the ravens. They should spare a thought for the many prisoners, like Sir Thomas More, held there without trial, waiting to know the King's or the Queen's pleasure, knowing they had little hope of leaving those grim walls alive.

In the spring of 1535, Parliament passed another Act of Treason. Now it was treason maliciously to refuse the King any of his titles, including that of Head of the Church, by wish, will or desire, by words or writing. There seemed no loophole; but Sir Thomas declared that he had done nothing *maliciously*. Witnesses were brought to accuse him of other crimes, such as taking bribes while he was in the King's service—although everyone knew Thomas More was almost the only man who had *not* done so.

In June, Bishop Fisher was taken from the Tower to Westminster to stand his trial for treason. Rich had tricked him into making a statement under a promise of secrecy. This was used in evidence against him. He was condemned to death, taken back to the Tower, and on June 22nd he was beheaded.

Then Sir Thomas More was taken from the Tower, and on July 1st he too stood trial in Westminster. He was still firm, and confident, for he knew that he had never said anything treasonable against the king.

'I do nobody harm, I say none harm, I think none harm, but wish everybody good. If this be not enough to keep a man alive in good faith, I long not to live,' he declared.

Then Richard Rich stood up to give evidence. He swore he had held a conversation with Sir Thomas, in which he had set out reasons for not taking the Oath. There was not a word of truth in it, but it was enough for the court's needs, and the King's purpose. More knew what it meant. He turned to Rich.

'I am sorrier for your perjury than for my own peril,' he said. Even now he could not be proved to have spoken *maliciously*—yet the court immediately returned a verdict of guilty. For the first time, More explained his meaning.

'No earthly Prince may presume to take upon himself, by any law, the spiritual authority of the See of Rome, which was given to St Peter and his successors by our Saviour himself,' he declared.

He was condemned to death, and the hideous details of the death ordered for traitors was read out. He was led away, in procession, the ceremonial axe with its blade turned towards him as a sign that he was condemned.

As the boat landed at the Tower, Meg forced her way through the crowds. The guards pushed her back, but she insisted and at last they let her through.

She knelt for her father's blessing and kissed him, not bearing to let him go, until the guards pulled her away.

That night he wrote to her from his cell, using a piece of coal, all the writing material he was allowed.

'I never liked your manner towards me better than when you kissed me last. Farewell my dear child and pray for me, and I shall for you and all your friends that we may merrily meet in Heaven.'

10. 'His merry death'

YEARS before, when he had written about the imaginary country of Utopia, Thomas More had spoken of the Utopians who were not Christians, but who went to their death calmly and readily. Their fellow citizens then cremated them, with songs of joy.

'And when they come home, they talk over his virtuous manners and his good deeds. But no part of his life is so oft or gladly talked of, as his merry death.'

Sir Thomas was determined that his Christian courage would not be put to shame by his own Utopians, and hoped to make his family and friends share in 'his merry death'.

The King, late in the day, showed him some mercy; he was to be beheaded with an axe, not submitted to all the savage torture inflicted on men condemned for treason. He was to be executed four days after his trial—the day chosen was July 6th, 1535.

When that day came, he was led from his cell through the Tower, and on to Tower Hill, where a crowd waited.

He had wanted to wear his best gown for the great occasion, but he was told his clothes would become the property of the executioner, so instead he put on a coarse grey gown that belonged to his servant.

The raised platform with the block set upon it was rickety, and he was unsteady after his long time in prison. 'I pray you, Master Lieutenant, see me safe up, and for my coming down, let me shift for myself!' he joked.

Like all condemned men, he was entitled to make a speech on the scaffold; but the King ordered that he should not speak for long. So he asked everyone to pray for him, and to bear witness that he suffered death for the sake of the Holy Catholic Church. Then he asked the bystanders to pray for the King, so that God would give him good counsel, and he declared that he died as the King's good servant, but God's first!

The executioner prepared to cover his eyes, but he said: 'I will cover them myself.' He tied a linen cloth over his face and calmly knelt down.

The executioner immediately raised the axe and struck off his head.

His body was buried in the Chapel of the Tower, known as St Peter ad Vincula. Some accounts say that it was later taken away and buried elsewhere, but it is hard to prove. It is probably still there in the Tower.

His head was stuck on a pike and displayed on London Bridge. But even now Margaret was still at hand, for what she considered her last grim duty. She managed to bribe the man in charge, and one dark night she took a boat to London Bridge. The head was thrown down from the bridge into her lap as she sat in the boat.

She preserved it in a casket, and took it out of London to be buried in Canterbury, the home of her husband's family, the Ropers.

King Henry ordered that Margaret should be arrested, and for a while she was in prison; but later she was released. She herself died nine years after her father.

11. *'God's servant first'*

WHEN Erasmus heard of More's death, he was overcome by grief. He wrote: 'In More's death I seem to have died myself; we had but one soul between us.'

Centuries later, Samuel Johnson, another great scholar, said: 'More was the person of the greatest virtue these islands ever produced.' And in our own day it has been said that the two greatest Englishmen who have ever lived have been William Shakespeare and Thomas More.

The Church he had died for recognised him more slowly. A hundred years after he died, an Englishman said: 'Methinks 'tis strange that all this time More is not canonised, for he merited highly of the Church.'

There were still three hundred years to wait!

At long last, in 1935, the 400th anniversary of their martyrdom, Thomas More and Bishop John Fisher were proclaimed as saints—heroic servants of God.

The Feast of Thomas More falls on July 6th, and we may pray to them to ask for their prayers. A church dedicated to the Holy Redeemer and St

Thomas More stands in Chelsea, on the land where More lived so happily with his family more than five hundred and fifty years ago; and many churches are dedicated to the English martyrs.

Thomas More was a great Londoner, born in the City, living in Chelsea, on trial at Westminster, imprisoned and executed in the Tower. Yet though Londoners never forgot him, they were slow to honour him with a statue. It came at last.

It stands on the Embankment at Chelsea. The seated figure of Thomas More looks out across the River Thames. Across his knees lies the golden chain of Lord Chancellor, as if he has just taken it off when he gave up that office. Round the base of the statue are the words:

SIR THOMAS MORE

1478=1535

SCHOLAR=STATESMAN=SAINT

The ceremony of unveiling the statue would have given Thomas More great pleasure and surprise. It took place on July 21st, 1969, the very day that Man first walked on the Moon, which is something More never thought of for his Utopia!

It was a great occasion, led by the Speaker of the House of Commons, and attended by the leaders of all the chief churches in Britain. In their speeches, they stressed the beliefs they shared, which included great admiration and thankfulness for Thomas More.

Mr Speaker declared: 'He died that we might worship God in our own way. He died that we might be free men and women.'

The Archbishop of Canterbury said: 'He believed that the Christian Church is a divine society wider than states and nations, and that duty to king yields place to duty to God'. The Cardinal Archbishop of Westminster stressed More's holy life, as well as his death. 'Men do not just become saints on the scaffold,' he pointed out.

And the Moderator of the Free Churches spoke for everyone when he said: 'This man of conscience, faithful to death, belongs to us all.'

The chapel in the Tower, where his body was buried and where probably it still lies, now has its own monument. Below a bust of More are the words:

THOMAS MORE

Knight=scholar=writer=statesman

Lord Chancellor of England 1529–32

Beheaded on Tower Hill, buried in this chapel

1535

Canonised by Pope Pius XI 1935.

Anyone who is interested in Thomas More may go and see these monuments.

Before More was made a saint, a Pope declared that More, along with Bishop Fisher and the other English martyrs, had died 'for God, for the Catholic Church, for justice and for truth'.

Such heroism did not end with Thomas More. In China at this time there are priests in prison because they will not give up their loyalty to the Pope.

Today, there are not many kings left. In most countries their powers have been taken over by a dictator, or by a group of men, who rule as harshly as King Henry VIII ever did. Their subjects are not allowed to speak or write freely, and any attempt to oppose them is punished by death or imprisonment.

The brave men and women who stand up to them, and are put in prison, are called Prisoners of Conscience. Most of them have no wish to destroy the government of their country, or to do it any harm. Yet they insist they must obey the voice of their own conscience that tells them human rulers must not be obeyed when what they command is wrong.

They can take Thomas More as their example, and echo his words, *'I am the state's good servant— but God's first!'*